Lovinia's Child

A Depression Tale

Barbara Venton Montgomery

HERITAGE BOOKS
2006

HERITAGE BOOKS
AN IMPRINT OF HERITAGE BOOKS, INC.

Books, CDs, and more—Worldwide

For our listing of thousands of titles see our website
at
www.HeritageBooks.com

Published 2006 by
HERITAGE BOOKS, INC.
Publishing Division
65 East Main Street
Westminster, Maryland 21157-5026

Other Heritage Books by the author:
Women Short-Changed by History
Wonderful "Wicked" Women of the World

International Standard Book Number: 978-0-7884-3360-1

For my beautiful twins, Melody and Melinda,
For my best friend, Viva,
For my faithful dog, Willie-Willie,
All gone away.

"It is hard to give an account of your life to men of another age than that in which you have lived."
Cato the Elder
(234-149 B.C.)

Chapter I

The future juvenile delinquents from 152nd Street, Calumet City. "Bub" is in the front row center at age three.

In the twenties and thirties, it was known as "Sin City" although the staid *Encyclopedia Britannica* called it "the strip" because it "attracted some notoriety." This was in Calumet City, Illinois—Cook County near the Indiana State line, next to Hammond, Indiana.

It was Al Capone's favorite place to cruise and it may have been the place where he contracted the syphilis that eventually killed him. The mob controlled "the strip" with its gaudy neon signs, cheap booze, strippers, con men, mobsters, and gypsies. It was a dangerous, degenerate place. For conventioneers looking for "fun" it was great. The mob also ran the strip and most of the city, which had a few "Mom and Pop" stores and more taverns per person than any other city in the world, according to *Ripley's Believe It or Not*. It was not the best place to raise a child.

The city took the name Calumet from the peace pipe of

the Indians who had been killed off two centuries previously. They would have been insulted or dishonored by the activities that went on in their old camping grounds. The peace pipe had been an object of veneration. It was smoked with tobacco, willow bark and sumac leaves, not with opium, marijuana, etc. To refuse the pipe was an insult. That was not a problem on State Street in Calumet City.

The rest of the town was grey, dreary, and poverty stricken. But not even the Great Depression dimmed the lights along "the strip." And the two Catholic Churches, St. Victor's and St. Andrew's, were busier than ever with the influx of sinners. The big Baptist Church on the other side of the state line was not welcoming to those in Calumet City. Its citizens might be contagious, with what, who knows.

The elementary school was crowded with dirty, smelly children who spoke the languages of Latvia, Russia, Transylvania, Lithuania, Ruthenia, the Ukraine, Germany, Estonia, Bulgaria, and Hungary. Refugees from the Great War, (the first one) drifted into South Chicago and out again, looking for a place to live and to find jobs. My mother, who taught fifth grade at Lincoln Elementary School, carried a bar of soap with her and threatened certain students (nicely) to use the bathtub in each facility before they could return to her classroom.

After my travels around the state as a foster child, it was good to have a mother again and a home, even in Calumet City. I had learned not to complain about anything. Now I complain about everything.

The "socially acceptable" residential section seventy years ago began with Elizabeth Street and covered seven blocks to the south of the forest preserve. We only went into the forest preserve with other children. It could be a dangerous place. At the far end of the forest preserve was Green Lake, which was supposed to be bottomless.

Sometimes at night you could hear the screaming of men.

Gunshots and flashlights were seen among the trees. No one ever called the police. The mob used the forest preserve to chastise and dispose of their own. Stolen cars and dead bodies were said to have been dumped in Green Lake.

Later, Cook County made the shallow end of the lake into a swimming pool. There was a rope across the water along Torrence Avenue. When we "ditched" school, we would go to Green Lake and the seniors would cool their beer in the deep end. If a badge came by, they would cut the rope tied to the beer, and all would disappear into the dark green water.

5

Beer was absolutely forbidden at school events and anyone, even adults, were subjects of Miss Jaack's nose. The smell of alcohol would have her calling the coach, and together they would expel the offender regardless of weight or age.

No student was permitted to have a car. A few parents drove their children to school, but during the Depression, who could afford the luxury of a car? Only the mob and the "Elliot Nesses." It was walk with friends or save up for a bicycle. As Miss Jaack's said, "Both were healthy activities."

The first big car, not a "Tin Lizzy," I can remember seeing in front of Zimmers was a big, long, black limousine that was slowly cruising down the street near Lincoln Elementary School.

"Who is that?" I asked Lorraine from next door. Lorraine was a skinny six-year old to my five. But she knew everything, including words I had never heard before. She tried to explain the word FUCK which was scrawled all over the neighborhood in Calumet City, including garage doors and curbs. She offered to demonstrate. Years later, my mother sent me a news clipping about a mother and daughter found by the police, mowed down at the breakfast table while finishing their coffee. The article indicated they might have been skimming from the prostitution ring they ran for the mob. So ended Lorraine and her mother.

"It's the mob, maybe Big Al," said Lorraine. Even I knew who that was. I could always read. Even those things children are not supposed to read. And listening to adults, I could put things together. The newspapers all over the state of Illinois had accounts of Al Capone's activities.

Especially graphic, were the stories of the St. Valentine's Day Massacre in 1929. Everyone knew that Capone was behind the killings, but he was never charged with "the massacre." After killing all of his rivals he was the supreme boss of Chicago and most of the suburbs, especially Cicero and Calumet City. He paid off police and judges. In South Chicago, in his big, black limo, his driver would drive slowly through the streets while he threw candy to the kids on their way home from school. He never did that in Calumet City.

The limo cruised on by. I saw the car several months later when Arnold, the Zimmers' son, and I were playing *hide and seek* in the hollyhocks in the back yard. My mother had retrieved me from a foster home in central Illinois, after she left the tuberculosis sanitarium. The only place she could afford to live in Calumet City was an attic with a German family. The Zimmers had escaped World War I by coming to the United States, but there was the stigma of being German in a community of Slavs, Croats and Eastern Europeans. Mr. and Mrs. Zimmer were wonderful to me. Mrs. Zimmer gave me my first dill pickle. There wasn't much to eat, but we always had dill pickles that she cooked up in the basement and there were fresh vegetables in the summer. Mr. Zimmer planted the vacant lot next door, then sat in the summer night with a big stick in his lap waiting for poachers.

When people are hungry and there was little on the shelf at Joe's Meat (?) Market, people stole anything they could for food. Mrs. Zimmer always had a weak cup of coffee and a piece of bread for the men who roamed the back alley going through the garbage cans. They would wash windows for her or weed the garden, but there was no sympathy for anyone who stole from Mr. Zimmer's garden.

The big, black limo was fascinating because there were so few cars between the strip and Elizabeth Street. Every now and again, Elliot Ness and the "still breakers" would park along the street near the Zimmers. They would come at dusk, get out of some old, beat-up car, sniff the air for alcohol fumes and haul out the axes and select a house to raid. It was that kind of neighborhood. A house with a fireplace was usually the target because the fumes could be vented up the chimney without fear of an explosion in the basement. His troopers, dressed in brown and gray baggy suits, never said much. And a police informant had usually warned their target that they were coming so no one was at home when they busted down the basement door. The operation was great fun to watch. We would yell when we heard the axes smashing the still.

The word would go out to the neighborhood:

"Free booze tonight!"

In the years of prohibition, this was good news. The alcohol was not sent streaming into the basement drain. That might cause one big explosion. This was volatile liquid. Instead it was drained down the driveway and into the street where eager neighbors waited with spoons and cups. Of course, "the booze" could make you blind, but it disinfected everything along the way and killed weeds, too. People could stay drunk a week after a raid, but some just up and died.

Mrs. Zimmer didn't want us to go outside when the raiders or the "Elliot Nesses" appeared.

Mr. Zimmer made his "bourbon" in the bathroom with the windows open. I don't know where he got the wood alcohol, but it almost ate away the bathtub tile.

"Come on, Bub. You can pour the vanilla and the syrup,

then take the bathtub plunger and stir it up good."

Mrs. Zimmer, who spoke more German than English, would come up the stairs yelling at her husband, and drag me out of the bathroom. She would sit me down at the kitchen table with one of Arnold's books and a dill pickle. Mrs. Zimmer favored learning even if her English was poor. She had a kind heart, but she didn't favor dealing with the mob and "bootlegged booze."

Later, when she was in the basement cooking, we would fill the milk bottles with our brew. In the morning, I would deliver it to the milkman and bring a cube of sugar for his horse. He would stash the bottles behind the milk and the ice. I received my reward—ice to slurp on. I then took more empty bottles upstairs to be filled with "bourbon."

Candy was an unknown quantity. I knew that other children sometimes bought it at a grocery store across Wentworth, but we had no money for this luxury. One day when I was taken into Chicago to see what was served in the big soup kitchen near Randolph Street, I encountered the real John D. Rockefeller. He was very, very old at the time and two male nurses who helped him get to his private train in the station accompanied him. As I came toward him, he motioned one of the men forward to meet me. His man gave me a dime, a real dime. He said something to me like, "make it grow."

I didn't know at that time who he was or what he meant. I took that dime back to Calumet City and went to the grocery store. I bought ten cents worth of candy and that was a lot of candy. I sat outside the store on the curb and ate all of that candy myself. Before I could get home to Zimmers I was sick, really sick, with all that sugar pouring into my half-starved tummy. I lost it all. If I had shared, I wouldn't have been sick. I learned a lesson.

***

The big, black limo returned to our street again. This time it was cruising the back alley and stopped behind Zimmer's garage. Big Al himself got out and put one foot on the running board of the limo so you could see his pearl gray spats.

He looked rich.

Capone had on a black suit, a white, white shirt and wore a light gray fedora with a black band. We weren't afraid of him, not exactly. It was more like awe. There was Al Capone in our alley!

Al was chewing on a cigar and looking around.

He spotted Arnold and me squatting in the hollyhocks.

We had been playing *hide-and-seek* on that hot afternoon. Most people were indoors, but it was cool under the fall flowers by the fence. We were also spying on the bully who lived behind us. We called him "Little Bruno." His father was "Big Bruno" and he worked for Al.

Arnold Zimmer was almost eight and I was almost five, but we were both small for our age. Arnold was my protector and keeper of the good books. He wasn't afraid of anything. I was afraid of everything, even caterpillars that scrunched along the back fence. "Little Bruno" said that he would eat off my fingernails when he caught me. He was a large 10 year-old, and he would chase me home from school.

Arnold Zimmer—protector, confidant, and mentor—with Bub when she lived with the Zimmers in Calumet City.

When Big Al spotted us, he looked threatening.

"You kids, get outta dose flowers. I wanna see what we

got here."

I promptly wet my panties and cried.

Big Al laughed when Arnold stood up.

"Get outta here. I don't shoot no babies."

That's when we saw the gun, not a little gun, but what was called a "Tommy Gun" by gangsters.

Arnold grabbed my hand and pulled me up, wet panties and all. It wasn't easy for him because I felt rooted in the hollyhocks.

Just then, Bruno came running out the back door. He had seen a black limo pull up in front, and he was going to escape his cohorts through the vacant lot and Mr. Zimmer's garden. But Al Capone was waiting with "The Thompson." He shot Bruno when he was half way to his garage. He just collapsed in a pile. Then Big Al got back into his limo and was driven casually down the alley. He never looked back at Arnold and me.

Bruno's body just lay there. It was so quiet that you could hear the flies buzzing around the blood in the driveway. We just sat there and watched Mrs. Bruno and her son, the bully, come outside. We were still squatting there when the police arrived. Then we crawled out of the flowers and hid in the basement. Finally, Mrs. Zimmer came looking for us.

We never told anyone what we had seen and no one ever asked us. Neither of us forgot that hot summer day. It was my first and only witness to a gangland killing.

We had known Bruno worked for the mob because his son boasted about it.

After the funeral, he and his mother moved, but the mob believed in giving their own a big send-off. That funeral was something to see. Arnold and I were again stationed in the hollyhocks. We saw almost every single black limo in Cook County, laden with sprays of flowers, pull up at Bruno's house. They lined up and down the street. This was the start of a procession through the streets of Calumet City and a tour of "the strip." It also served as a warning: "Don't cross Al Capone! What did Bruno do to deserve the killing?" We never knew—probably skimming from gambling or prostitution.

After that, the only thing killed for a while was a mean looking dog, run over by the "Elliott Nesses" in their search for illegal booze. The dog didn't remain in the street very long because people were hungry. The year was 1931 and the depression was beginning to set in. Across the street, renting a back room in the Novak house, lived Jimmy-the-Greek. What else? He was a real entrepreneur with a three-stool restaurant on the street in Hammond. When he closed his lean-to at night, he brought home leftovers for all the kids in the neighborhood. No one ever asked what was in the stew he made. It was good, hot, and possibly dog.

As the depression deepened, men began standing around the corner by the meat (?) market feeding sticks into an oil drum and growling about the government, no jobs, no food, and no money. Some of them left their families and "rode the rails" in freight trains that came through the yards in Hammond. Some of them just disappeared. Every now and again my mother would get a railroad pass from an uncle who worked on the old Illinois Central Line. We would travel south to Belknap where another uncle had a farm. We would carry corn, potatoes and cucumbers (dill pickles) back to the Zimmers with the assistance of the conductors along the way. My mother always gave them some of our pickings, so they helped us with the burlap bags. Some of them I knew from my days in foster care.

"Here's our little gal again," they would call to each other down the train. They had always fed me candy, cakes, sandwiches and anything in their black lunch boxes. Of course, I became sick because I wasn't used to all of that food, especially sweets. Someone would be waiting for me in Watseka, Momence, Herrin, Harrisburg or Gilman. As I was lifted down the train steps, on cue, I would throw-up.

Not a good thing for a foster child living on someone's sufferance.

How did I get so lucky to be in Calumet City again with my mother? So begins my tale.

Chapter II

Bub and her father, Francis, in Wateka on one of the very few occasions she saw him after he left his wife and child in Calumet City. Francis looked like F. Scott Fitzgerald, drank like him, and womanized like him.

That afternoon, in the winter of 1928, my father left the house and my life forever. For a child, this was complete rejection and devastating. I sat on the sofa and watched him go from bedroom to living room and to his beat-up college steamer trunk with University of Illinois stickers on it. He never said a word as he moved back and forth. My mother was in the kitchen crying softly. What had I done to make my mother and father act this way?

This is how I remember my father who was about to depart with a rather dumpy beautician, so I later learned. I met Bernice once when my father took me to her house where she "marcelled" my hair, hurriedly, so she could join my father in the bedroom. My mother cried when she saw the blisters on my scalp and my burned hair. I did have frizzy hair, which I liked, until my mother cut it all off.

Up until my father's departure, all I can remember

about this period of my life was the smell of stale beer, sitting in my high chair half the night because I refused to eat peas and a trip to a speakeasy where my father knocked three times and said, "Francis," to a disembodied ghost behind a door. There was also an incident at a party which involved wife swapping.

I was put into a big bed with ladies coats stacked on it. It was warm and comforting under fur and wool. A couple came into the dark room and saw me "sleeping" under the coats. "If she wakes up, I swear I'll kill the little brat."

I didn't move until they did their thing and left. Then I slept until morning. Someone had carried me home. It may have been Francis, but it wasn't my mother. She had begun hemorrhaging and trying to deny the tuberculosis that ran in her family.

***

Before my father's departure, we first lived in a one-room basement apartment that was always gloomy. Then we moved to a small duplex near Lincoln School in Calumet City where my mother hoped to get a job teaching. Something must have happened in the basement that caused our sudden move to that duplex, because I was always frightened. If someone looked at me, I wet my panties. I wet the bed, I wet the floor, but seldom did I wet in the toilet. I was worse than the most ill trained puppy.

The duplex was one half of a depression bungalow. There was little furniture, which included my high chair, an ancient brown sofa, a small kitchen table and several chairs. The speckled linoleum was cracked in several places. I know because I tried to help my mother scrub the floor. It was an ugly house.

Maybe this was why my father left us there, but I believe it was for Bernice, the dumpy beautician.

My mother was taken away late one night when I was sick. I heard her cry and got out of bed to find the bathroom covered with blood. She struggled with the ambulance attendants until the Olsons came from next door to take care of me. I didn't see her again for many months. And she did not come back for me until I was seven or eight. I thought she had left me forever.

The Olsons had rented the second half of the duplex. They came to my rescue that night and wanted desperately to adopt me. They even went to the judge and begged him to consider their request. They had no children. Mr. Olson was a big, round Swede and she was a tall, slim Italian. They were the first in a series of interesting people who took care of me until my mother reclaimed me.

Foster care was not regulated too well in Cook County,

Illinois during the depression. Usually the only mandatory requirement was that the foster family took the child to church, any church. By the time I was sixteen, I had been to them all, even the snake handlers down in the church basement. I had nightmares about snakes for years.

The Olsons were Catholic and took me to St. Victor's. This was my introduction to Christianity. I loved the incense, the candles and the sound of Latin. I always fell asleep before the service was over, but they didn't care. I would play with Mrs. Olson's rosary and drift off. Mr. Olson would carry me home. I sometimes heard him praying that they could keep me. I did not wet their bed until the trial to see who could have me. I remember the courtroom, the judge, my grandparents, (not my father) my sick mother with her father, and the big chair I climbed into to "testify."

The court doesn't do this to children anymore, I hope.

I cried, wet my panties, and never did testify.

The Olsons were glad for my mother when she won and with a tearful good-by, they moved to St. Louis. They were good to me. I never saw them again.

My mother disappeared into the sanitarium again just before Christmas when I was four years old. My grandfather came from Watseka and took me home for the most wonderful Christmas of my life. Every child should have such a memory of Christmas to cherish. I stood in awe of what only Santa could create.

The tree stood in the "day" room, hidden behind large glass doors. When Aunt Barbara opened the doors, there it was, a gleaming, incredible work of art, with lights and ornaments. On a sea of white surrounding the tree were big boxes and little boxes. All for me.

Of course, I cried and wet my panties, but no one scolded me. Instead, my grandmother hugged me and we went up to the white bedroom and changed my panties. After Christmas, we bought some new panties, dresses and socks and something frilly, with lace, like a slip.

Jimmy Ringer, Bub's neighbor in Wateka. Bub planned to marry Jimmy when she was five year's old but changed her mind at six. She felt that he was not mature enough for her. Jimmy was killed in World War II at the Battle of the Bulge.

I had arrived at their home with a dress that was too short, two pairs of dirty panties, a sweater that was too little and sandals that showed all five toes.

The year was 1929. I stayed with my grandparents from Christmas through summer. It was a happy time. Jimmy Ringer was my next door neighbor and a year older than I. We played together making daisy chains for each other, crowning ourselves with flowers. We drank lemonade that his mother made and ate grapes from the arbor. Some afternoons, Grandmother would dress me up in my new clothes and we would go calling on all of her friends. I learned how to sip tea without spilling it, use a napkin and not stuff cookies in my mouth, all at one time. We walked the tree-lined streets and said "hello" to everyone.

People said, "What a charming child." I was four years old and wet the bed only once.

Then came that black Friday in September when my world in Watseka ended.

It would be many years before I understood the impact of "the crash" of 1929 and the Great Depression that followed. But for my grandparents, it was catastrophic.

When Grandfather came into the house late that afternoon, he announced to the house,

"It's gone, everything in gone." And he collapsed.

Four generations: L to R—Great Grandmother Crossland, Grandmother Gilbreath, Bub and Mother. Mother seems so young and happy in the picture, reminiscent of the girl in her high school yearbook that fellow students called "the vamp." Her ambition at seventeen was to be the favorite wife in a harem.

He meant all the money that he had put away had disappeared with a poker-playing buddy, the bank president. He just left town with all of the bank's money, some said to South America. There was not a penny anywhere in Watseka. Some of Grandfather's friends killed themselves. One threw himself in front of the afternoon Illinois Central train. Another jumped from the fourth floor of the only hotel in town.

I learned later that my grandparents' two daughters came to Watseka to help Grandmother. My father never appeared. His sisters were blond, blue-eyed Pearl, Ashkenazi, and dark-haired, brown-eyed Barbara, Sephardic, for whom I was named, I guess. They both married very well, but they seemed to be jealous of each other, especially Aunt Barbara. She was always condescending to everyone, especially me, and was always making excuses for my father who did not support me, nor did he want to.

My grandfather often said that his daughters had been educated beyond their intelligence.

I was quickly removed from the house by two "ancient aunts" who lived on the other side of the town. I didn't even know I had "ancient aunts." They were my mother's, mother's sisters, the "other side" of the family. They said that they would keep me until my mother's sister or someone could pick me up and care for me. I didn't see my grand-parents again for four years after that terrible day, even though we lived in the same small town.

By this time I had forgotten what my father looked like although his parents had shown me pictures of him. Some said that he looked exactly like F. Scott Fitzgerald and drank like him, too. In college, he was quite the ladies man, before, during and after my mother.

My great uncle was Thomas Arkle Clark, the first dean at the University of Illinois. When he presented the diplomas at graduation, he spotted my father among the graduates. "My God, Gilbreath, how did you get here?"

In contrast to my father's academic record, my mother was a scholarship student who had her pick of several colleges. But she had room and board at the University of Illinois because of Uncle T. A. Her roommate was the sister of Emiliano Aguinaldo, a hero of the Filipino Independence movement. Aquinaldo had lost his fight for a republic after the United States navy captured Manila in 1898. He came on board an U.S. warship under a flag of truce to effect a cease-fire. The U.S. was chauvinistic then and the ship sailed away with him on board. Some of his family were picked up as hostages and ended up in Illinois, the central

27

part of the United States. They received a college education in exchange for their freedom. Aguinaldo's sister never told my mother if the deal was worth it. She gave my mother a gift of an embroidered table set for her wedding, which I now have. Uncle T. A. became the dean of foreign students and was invited to Japan to set up a university before World War I.

Uncle T. A. enjoyed removing wayward students from the University and went on raids with the campus police. He never caught my father. But he did catch James Reston, a famous columnist, who wrote a column on how to get kicked out of college, especially by Uncle T. A. Even my mother's doctor in Texas, Sherman Sparks, along with Reston, wanted to be teachers. They said Uncle T. A. gave them a new sense of direction when he escorted them to Illinois Central out of Urbana and personally saw they were on their way north. Unfortunately, he did not help my father. Since Uncle T. A. was from my mother's side of the family, he did not approve of their marriage. There was constant warfare on both sides of the family. When the marriage ended (no one ever said the word divorce) in 1929, I was left to the orders of Judge Posanski's court and whomever would take a dispossessed child left fatherless and whose mother was in a sanitarium.

In all of my wandering around the state, my paternal Grandmother always knew where I was and sent me small gifts, or had my aunt Barbara do it, for my birthday or Christmas. She sent me small hand knit mittens after I was in high school, but the thought of "Little Barbara" was always there.

Grandmother Gilbreath was Jewish. Before World War II there was violent anti-Semitism in Illinois. I was unaware that her kitchen was kosher. We went to the Methodist Church on Sunday. There were no other Jews in town. Her father was dead and her sister, Aunt Jessie, lived in Florida. She too, had married well. The secret of the Jewish family was kept so well that I did not know about her parents until I visited Aunt Jessie's house in Florida after her death. There in the attic were picture albums of dead relatives and friends. In one of those albums was a small man wearing a yarmulke and his equally small, smiling wife. When I asked who they were, Aunt Barbara said that they were my great grandparents from Lorraine. I asked why he was wearing a yarmulke and if I could have a picture of them?

"No!" The album disappeared.

I do have several pictures of my grandmother but not the one I wanted. That picture showed Grandmother sitting on the front row of a high school graduation class holding a diploma in her fist. Serious young men who were trying not to smile surround her.

All three of her children graduated from college, but no one knew they were Jewish or the girls could not have pledged their sorority at the University.

I saw my first parade with my Grandfather. He was intensely patriotic. He was too young for the Civil War, but he had his father's medals displayed in a prominent place in the library. One was for bravery on the field of battle and the other one was given to him at Gettysburg by Abraham Lincoln for bravery in that engagement. I always wanted to wear one of them to show that I was brave, too.

Wherever the flag was paraded, Grandpa would say, "Get up, Bub, that's our flag."

My father had Grandfather's permission to enter the Navy in 1917. He was on a troop ship going to France when a German submarine torpedoed it. Only two men survived and one was my father. All of the other men were lost in the Atlantic. My father came home something of a hero, from which he never recovered. He went to the University for the first homecoming where he met my mother. Incidentally, universities in the United States are beholden to Uncle T. A. for the institutions of Homecoming and Dad's Day. He is also said to be responsible for the first Japanese University in Hokkaido, Japan. At one time my mother had a pale blue Kimono with pink flowers presented to him by the Emperor of Japan. Unfortunately the moths got it before I did. Uncle T. A. also spoke to the Prince of Wales, later Edward VIII, while washing the windows of the girls' dormitory in his white suit, white shirt and black string tie. He was something of a character.

Although Uncle T. A. did not approve of my father, he did like my Grandfather Gilbreath who was superintendent of Education in Iroquois County. He was also a teacher and a good politician. Before that terrible day in 1929 he would take me to political rallies. I would pass out campaign literature and say, "Vote for my Grandpa," in a loud voice. I loved the crowds, the cheering and all of those people smiling at me. When we would come home late at night, I would sleep in the back seat of his Pontiac on top of campaign literature.

Grandfather's father, Hiram Gilbreath, was from the island of Gigha, off the Mull of Kintyre, Scotland. I found it to be a mystical place where the ancestors defeated the *Giants* (probably Vikings) who came in Dragon ships. All the gravestones on Gigha indicate teachers and sailors who left the islands to seek new worlds. They are centuries old, but older still are the weird shaped megaliths, placed there when the island emerged from the glacial water by prehistoric man.

Of course, Grandfather wrote poetry and drank Scotch.

***

After the court battle over my custody, the Polish-Catholic Judge Pozanski, a Democrat, certainly would not award me to a Jewish grandmother and a Scottish politician who happened to be a Republican office holder.

Then there was my mother's family. My mother's mother had died in childbirth. She came from early Illinois settlers arriving by Conestoga wagons. Good Anglo-Irish stock, I was told.

I met my Grandpa Crawford only once after I left the "ancient aunts." His sister, my Aunt Rose, drove from her farm near Watseka to Southern Illinois to see him and she took me along.

Grandpa Crawford's house was on a hill overlooking the spur of the Ozarks. The Shawnee loved this place. I slept on a pallet of goose feathers causing me to have an asthma attack, but I didn't wet the feathers. In the morning, he took me to the pasture that was within walking distance of the house. When they heard him whistle, the horses came thundering up the hill from the small stream at the bottom of the pasture.

At the age of four, the horses looked to me to be untamed and wild, tossing their manes and snorting, vying for carrots and sugar from his hand. Many years later, I realized they were all old nags, wheezing and swinging their heads for more air. But that summer morning, they belonged to the gods. Especially to my Grandfather who loved and cared for them in their old age. They were a given to him as he traveled each spring through the hill country of Southern Illinois, across the river at Shawneetown and into Kentucky, bringing clothing, food and the benefits of marriage and baptism to the "Lost Shawnee." This was after white settlers proclaimed that they had eliminated all Indians from the Kentucky shore. But we are still there, a migratory people who love the land.

In his obituary, no mention is made of his ancestry. Since history is "the myth agreed upon by historians," my aunt, who was in her nineties finally told me his story. His parents were killed in Ohio. When word came of *Custer's Last Stand* in 1876, he was placed in the workhouse as a child. I found him listed in the Dallas Public Library. A Methodist minister took him to Hoopeston, Illinois, a college town, where he and his sister received an education. When asked by the minister about his parents, he promptly said, "Mary and Joseph." This made such an impression on the minister that he took Rose and Joseph home with him.

A decade later, he went to Watseka to court my grandmother Cynthia. She was beautiful. Her pictures show her to be tall and patrician looking. Of course he was shorter, dark and square-jawed. A determined Shawnee who had an education, but was quite unacceptable to her mother and to her brother, Uncle Ed. So they ran off to southern Illinois where they married and he founded the town of Belknap, several miles south of Marion. He built a house nearby and a drawbridge over a stream.

Since her father had been lost in the gold rush, (at least that was what I was told) Uncle Ed had taken charge of the situation. He was the town lawyer (one reason I don't like lawyers) and member of the Women's Temperance Union. He never did anything except turn off the new electricity and complain about money. He was known as the stingiest man in town.

After coming home from lawyers' convention in Chicago, he informed everyone that he had been impulsive and had married into French aristocracy. When Lady Claire finally arrived in Watseka by one of the two paved roads, she hated it on sight. She needed a more fanciful existence and she certainly wasn't going to get it with Uncle Ed. I remember when she sailed into town and out again on one of her sporadic visits with several "courtiers" in attendance.

If it meant money, she wasn't going to get it from Uncle Ed. To a child, she didn't look royal. She was fat, over-dressed, snooty and demanding. I did improve my table manners after watching her. She stuffed her face until her cheeks puffed out like a happy chipmunk. How could she swallow all that food? I knocked over my milk and dumped the sugar bowl as I watched her stow away all of that food. Great Grandmother went to her bedroom.

Even when *the royal* left town after eating everything in sight and demanding a divorce from Uncle Ed, who didn't seem particularly devastated, he still acted as if he were a representative to the non-existent French court.

***

Back in Belknap, my mother was the first-born, then came Auntie Mae, Uncle John and Aunt Bonnie. Grandmother had died in childbirth and at age nine, my mother was given the responsibility for the children. She carried them on her hips until she got rheumatic fever. The doctor forbade any more lifting when he discovered she had a permanently displaced right hip.

Relatives from Watseka came to claim Aunt Bonnie, but Grandpa hid her and accused them of attempted kidnaping. Since he was mayor, judge and chief of police in

Belknap, Uncle Ed retreated. But he saw to it that we were all disinherited "unto the third and fourth generation."

Because of his education, Grandpa was often called upon to marry people or bury them; so he set up his own funeral parlor and worked with several local carpenters to make coffins. My mother described playing hide-and-seek in and out of the coffins. When customers came to purchase a casket, the kids were told to play

Grandfather Gilbreath and Bub reading the newspaper and sharing opinions on the sate of the country before "the crash" of 1929.

near the storm cellar or the icehouse. Of course, it happened that one day my mother and Auntie Mae were hiding in the coffins when a family of four came to see what was available for their deceased. When they opened the second coffin in a row, out popped Auntie Mae who had put white baking powder on her face to "look dead." The two women fainted immediately, but when my mother popped up out of

36

her satin lined setting, the men ran. Good thing that Grandpa had a sense of humor. He told that story for years.

Grandpa could be counted on to give a wonderful eulogy. If you were a storyteller or had a way with words, in all of "little Egypt," you were said to have "Crawford's gift." Grandpa was asked to settle disputes, referee baseball games and host housewarmings. Like the great Shawnee chief, Tecumseh, some of his descendants predict earthquakes and the dates of their deaths.

He came to Chicago to help my mother in the court battle to retain custody of me until she could leave the tuberculosis sanitarium. He convinced Judge Pozanski that she would be able to return and care for me, although I remained a ward of the court until I was twenty-one.

Grandfather Gilbreath presenting Bub with her first puppy named Spot. Then they all went campaigning to Mommence. Grandfather ran and was elected superintendent of public schools in Iroquois County for many years.

Grandpa died when I was eight. My mother had indeed reclaimed me and I was living with her and her new husband, Charles.

We went to Belknap and to the house on the hill. The horses he had loved were gone.

Someone said, "Gone to the glue factory."

He would have wept for them.

Chapter III

Three generations:: L to R—Mother, Grandmother, Cynthia Crawford, who died in childbirth, and Auntie Mae.

Ah, the "ancient aunts," an odd pair to rescue a child. They didn't like their brother, Uncle Ed, either. They took me back across town (all of five blocks). When great-grandmother wanted a picture of five generations, the aunts returned me for two hours with a promise that there would be children with which to play. I looked forward to this.

However, the boys tied me to a big oak tree in front of the house and poked me with stick shouting, "Scalp the little Indian."

Someone knew about Grandpa Crawford and had gossiped in the neighborhood. Probably Uncle Ed.

Great Grandmother appeared in a long lace dress and high-topped, laced black shoes and ordered Uncle Ed to untie me. She wiped away my tears and gave me a lump of sugar.

Then the "ancient aunts" took me back to their little

bungalow and put me to bed. Jackie Brown joined me and we fell asleep together. Jackie was the best-loved member of the household. He was a sweet old dog who was stuffed with more food than most families ate in a week during the depression. He usually slept under the cooking stove, so he ate often.

Jackie was named for Aunt Julia's husband, Police Chief Jack Brown, who died under somewhat mysterious circumstances. His death was not investigated with the forensics available today.

Chief Brown was reputed to have a bad temper, especially when he had been drinking. He was known to have beaten prisoners from the wrong side of town, and may have whacked Aunt Julia, too. She was the only woman among both families who was inclined to be quiet and mousy. He sometimes chased her son, Leslie, and Jackie Brown around the house, threatening to finish them off.

Anyway, he came in late one Friday night demanding his supper. Aunt Julie and Aunt Viola, who was visiting at the time, along with Leslie and Jackie Brown, took refuge in the root cellar. Sometimes in the summer, Jackie slept on the top step of the cellar where it was cooler. As Chief Brown began looking for the family, he opened the door to the cellar and slid off the back of Jackie, whose howls could be heard down the block. Head first, Chief Brown fell down the stairs and his gun went off. The police were called and they found their chief at the bottom of the stairs with a bullet right between his eyes.

The neighbors said that they heard several shots, but no one questioned Jackie Brown as to his whereabouts. A new police chief was appointed and the incident was quickly forgotten. Aunt Julia took to her bed and Aunt Vi took over.

She stayed in Watseka for several months to "settle things" and Jackie Brown lived a pampered life until he died of old age at 21.

Aunt Vi and Uncle Jim then moved to Washington, D.C. to a large apartment behind the Dutch Embassy. Of course, Aunt Vi made forays to Illinois in order to keep everyone, including a U.S. Senator, in line and to look after the Cary farms and grain elevator. She dispensed money to the deserving, young Billie Graham and Senator Dirkson, whom she said, "Voted like I told him." She bought a job in the local pharmacy for Leslie Brown who really had a degree but did not believe in work. He bought a new Ford with a "rumble seat" which he drove at a high rate of speed through the cornfields, sometimes with me singing to the birds. Helen Brown, Aunt Julia's daughter and Aunt Vi's favorite, bought hundreds of shoes in which I clomped around until my feet got too big for her size five shoes.

Aunt Vi did not believe my Grandpa Crawford's relatives had any potential. She tipped waiters lavishly if they told her they were working to get enough money for the University. She relented a little when my cousin, Anna Lou, graduated from high school. Since Ann and I were obviously not college material, Ann was invited to a summer in Washington D.C., but Auntie Mae said Ann couldn't go without me. It was a fantastic trip for a high school sophomore who loved history.

The only problem we had was Aunt Vi's determination to marry Ann off at seventeen, so she would have a place in society. The object she had selected for Ann was a dim-witted millionaire who was a ward of her husband's. He lived in the other apartment on our floor. The only activity that interested him was croquet. His croquet set was carefully placed on the apartment house lawn with a small fence around it. Ann hated the sight of him. I resolved the situation by beating him at his own game. He had a fit, (really a fit!) jumping up and down, frothing at the mouth and breaking his croquet mallet. He was carted off to the hospital. Ann and I were sent back to Illinois in disgrace.

So I worked three jobs at the university: once as a model for the portrait painting class. I hang in the N.Y.

Metropolitan Museum as the ship captain's daughter in a plaid shirt and my hair in braids. I also worked as a *Daily Illinois* editor, and as a cashier in the Union lunchroom, where I even short-changed the university president.

I got to class enough to graduate without Aunt Vi's help.

If I thought I would get a graduation card from Aunt Vi, I was wrong. She and Uncle Jim had both graduated from the University. She made straight A's in Chemistry and managed food services at several hospitals. Uncle Jim became a tax lawyer for the government and practiced before the Supreme Court. He always carried $25,000 in his briefcase, so he could buy up farmland before it was sold at auction. He also collected emeralds for Aunt Vi. Where he found emeralds in the Depression in rural Illinois, no one knew but Uncle Jim. Aunt Vi wore emerald rings mounted with diamonds on eight fingers. She promised one ring to each of the cousins, but they all disappeared before her death.

When she married Uncle Jim, her first cousin, they decided not to take a chance having offspring. She had no children of her own to command, so she told the relatives how to bring up their children.

When she died in Watseka at age 103, she found a way

to take it with her, aided by an unscrupulous attorney.

Helen died in the 1970s without children.

Leslie died before Helen, without children.

The emeralds are probably in some lawyers vault or with one of Helen's several husbands.

Next door to the "ancient aunts" lived a black lady who made cookies for me and told me stories while the aunts napped. She was a descendant of Thomas Jefferson. She showed me his inkwell presented to him by "a grateful Congress" and his hand-made eye glasses (bifocals). I was visiting her when people came from Monticello to restore his things to the plantation house. I hid behind her skirts when she opened the door for the two women and a man. When they saw the color of her skin, they almost fell off the porch. They got back into the car and drove off. Then we had lemonade and cookies, and she promised me a slice of apple pie later.

What happened to these precious things of Thomas Jefferson? I never doubted that the lady of the cookies was Jefferson's descendant by way of Sally Hemmings. Years later, while filming a documentary at Monticello, I saw the glasses and the inkstand again. I wondered how they got there and knew that the lady of the cookies had found a way.

*** *

The "ancient aunts" stated emphatically that I was not welcome for Christmas. What could they do with a precocious five year-old who could learn history by consorting with their black neighbors? Also, my first gift of a book was from a black railroad conductor on the Illinois Central who held a degree from Tuskegee. It was a biography of Elizabeth I. My mother later took it away. She thought it was "too advanced" for me and felt I should play with dolls, which I never did.

I was picked up in Watseka that Christmas, by a chauffeur for Mr. Layer who lived in Gilman. It was 1930 and jobs couldn't be had, especially by college graduates. Bud Heren had known my mother in college and had visited her in the sanitarium. In despair, she asked him if he could get me to Auntie Mae's in Herrin. She had no money for a train ticket and I couldn't stay in Watseka.

Bud went to Mr. Layer with the problem and it was solved. I would stay in Gilman until after Christmas, then Bud would put me on the train to Carbondale where someone would meet me.

Mr. Layer was an old bachelor—stone deaf and retired with lots of money from his food concessions on Mexican railroads before the Revolution. His big Airdale, wildly barking, would let him know when people came to the front door. The house would vibrate and pictures fall off the walls. Mr. Layer also owned the pharmacy in Gilman. It was a fascinating place. He made me my first butterscotch sundae and lime coke. I was spoiled forever. His assistants sold cosmetics, perfumes, cough medicines, crayons, magazines, candles and Christmas tree ornaments. He used real candles on his Christmas tree, never fearing that neither the dog nor I would topple it and set the house on fire.

What a wonderful house, almost as big as Grandfather Gilbreath's house in Watseka. The books-to-the-ceiling library smelled of leather and spicy pipe smoke.

The kitchen was decorated with Mexican tile and colorful fruit from Mexico that I had never tasted before. I loved Mexico before I ever resided there.

I had my own bedroom with a potty seat and a bed big enough for six people. I never wet the bed at Mr. Layer's house. It was a comforting and secure place. He was a kind man.

The dog and I claimed the backyard. We made snow angels and rolled in the snow. Mr. Layer loved flowers. That Christmas, poinsettias lined the stairs and the entrance hall. I went with him as he decorated churches in town with candles and flowers and carried medicine and baskets of food to the elderly. He looked like Santa with his round smiling face and a fringe of white hair. He radiated good will.

It was in his library that I became a reader, although I could read before I arrived at his home. Every evening we would sit in a big leather chair before the fire and read together. Any book I chose was the selection of the evening. After that Christmas in Gilman, I could read anything and I was never alone because I always had a book with me.

When it was time for Bud to take me to the train for Southern Illinois, I cried and so did Mr. Layer. Whenever we visited Watseka, I demanded to see my friend in Gilman. He died when I was at the university. I had been sending him funny little figurines when he was in the hospital.

He was the first person I knew for sure was in my corner.

Lovinia's Child: A Depression Tale

Chapter IV

Bub greeting her constituencies from the steps of Grandmother Gilbreath's front porch before presenting her calling cards at afternoon tea in Watseka.

After Christmas, I went to Auntie Mae in Herrin. I secretly prayed that Mr. Layer would adopt me, but of course, that couldn't happen. By this time I had completely forgotten my mother in the sanitarium and a father who didn't want me. I was part of a family. There was Auntie Mae, Uncle Maple, and their daughter, my beloved Anna Lou (Ann), and all of the women and girls who were always around gossiping, listening to the radio and singing.

Most of the women on my mother's side of the family could sing, I couldn't. My cousin Ann was the most sharing person in my life. She shared not only her candy, but also her bicycle. She would pump away with me on the seat, and we would travel all over Herrin. We jumped rope, played jacks and she shared her friends and her secrets with me. She sang on the radio, in the adult church choir, at school events, weddings and funerals. She was better than any of the popular singers of the day and she could imitate them all. When she went to song practice, I went too.

She would tell me, "Be a good mouth-mover, Bub." This was sixty years before Karioki. For every popular song in twenty years, I knew the lyrics. Several of her records of gospel music were played at her funeral in 1994.

Ann was popular in spite of Uncle Maple, although she did not have a real date until her senior prom. She was allowed to go to state band competitions, where she played clarinet, but was not allowed to sleep overnight with friends.

When I was older and visited Auntie Mae in Herrin, people mistook me for Ann, and I was flattered. We both have hazel eyes, olive skin, skinny nose and prominent cheekbones. We look like we belong to the Shawnee Nation except for light brown hair.

I was usually terrified of Uncle Maple. He looked like the Magua Mr. Layer had read about in *The Last of the Mohicans*. He was probably pure Iroquois. There was a soft violence in him. The little boys in the neighborhood called his mama "squaw woman." She would chase them with a tomahawk when they ran through her yard yelling,

"Squaw, squaw, dirty old squaw."

It made for an exciting afternoon in Herrin.

Uncle Maple had jet-black hair; black eyes and a smile

like a grinning shark. He worked in the coal-mines near Carbondale. His skin was dark and the coal dust made it look darker. He could never scrub the coal dust off. He died of that coal dust in his lungs, compounded by the mustard gas used by the Germans in the Great War to save Democracy. He also marched into Washington D.C. in 1932 in the Bonus Army demanding early payment of their veterans' pensions. Traveling in a freight train boxcar, he camped with the army near the Capitol. President Hoover refused to meet with the veterans. Instead, he sent federal troops, led by Douglas MacArthur, George Patton and Dwight Eisenhower to set the camp afire and to get rid of the Bonus Army. Uncle Maple hated Republicans.

He loved Auntie Mae and Ann and tolerated me. With his first check from the mine, he moved them from a boxcar on the railroad siding near Belknap into a small frame house across from his mother in Herrin. There were "no toilet facilities," so I carried a "slop jar" around because I still wet the bed.

Ann's cot was too small for both of us so I slept on a pallet by their big bed. One night Uncle Maple got up not knowing I had wet the bed. The urine had seeped on to the floor making it slippery. Of course he slipped in it and I learned my second bad word:

"Oh shit," he yelled as he went sliding into the kitchen.

"No it's not; its only pee, Maple," was Auntie Mae's sleepy reply.

We spent the next morning outside washing sheets. I learned to use the scrub board and lye soap that burned my hands. We used a heavy stick to catch the sheets after boiling rinse water was poured into one of the big wash tubs. I liked the morning outside with the clean white sheets. When the rinse water-cooled, Ann and I got our weekly bath. Right there in the backyard without a stitch of clothing, for all the world to see how clean we were. Afterward, we would split a sucker with candy at both ends of the stick.

We each had a job to do. Ann cleaned the house, (she was eight) Auntie Mae took in washing and sewed for ladies. Uncle Maple worked in the mines, and I did dishes and mixed the margarine. It was really lard, sometimes it was rancid because that was the cheapest, and sometimes the store gave it away. I had to stir in the red powder, which made it yellow. There was only one problem: the smell of rancid lard made me violently sick. Butter is butter, and it may be forming cholesterol, but never set margarine before me. I can smell the difference from two feet away.

Bologna was another disliked remnant of the

Depression. Auntie Mae would fry it, bake it, mix it into casseroles, but no way could I eat it. We had fresh vegetables, too, that Auntie Mae grew along with sweet peas. There were flowers on the table all summer. Sometimes Uncle Maple "found" a chicken.

One night he took us to see a traveling minstrel show that featured a "Medicine Man" who sold the "elixir of life." It was almost as pure alcohol as the brew I would make with Mr. Zimmer. When the *Hoochy-Koochy* girls began gyrating, Auntie Mae took us home with a warning to Uncle Maple. Much, much later, he came home, having met with "old buddies."

I could hear whispered words like "scabs, night riders, run them out of town, don't forget the massacre" (Herrin Massacre) and "not my sheets, you don't," from Auntie Mae. That usually ended the discussion and it was quiet in Herrin that night. The medicine show moved on the next day.

Auntie Mae took me to the sanitarium to see my mother when the doctors decided that she wasn't contagious any more. It had been more than a year since she went away. The sanitarium was a long white building with a wide veranda where patients could sit in the sunshine or receive visitors on Sunday. When the attendants wheeled a smiling lady to the grass where Auntie Mae had spread a quilt, I bolted. The attendant caught me, I screamed, and wouldn't let my mother hug me or touch me. I cried; she cried; and the attendant wheeled her away. Auntie Mae was devastated and kept saying, "It will be alright, you'll see," to herself and to me. I always felt as many children do, that I was the reason my father left, and I caused my mother's health to deteriorate when I was born.

***

Uncle Maple planned a treat: homemade peach ice cream. He had been given an ice cream maker with a crank handle and a set of instructions for making ice cream. I wanted to help, but Auntie Mae had polished the floor, and I tripped over the sliding throw rug falling into the ice cream maker, turning it over. Ice cream, still in the unfrozen stage fell all over the floor and ruined the operation. Uncle Maple smiled his Maqua smile, white, white teeth and cold black eyes. He took off his belt with a solid silver buckle and came after me. Auntie Mae screamed, Ann screamed, I howled, and went flying through the house. I crawled under the daybed on the porch. It was hot and close, bad enough, but Ann sat on the bed with her legs over the side to hide me and bounced up and down.

"Out, out," called Uncle Maple and he too sat on the

bed, pinning me underneath. I'm sure the whole neighborhood could hear me screaming. I had been warned the night I arrived about Uncle Maple's temper and the belt. I had tried to be good, but Lord, my death was at hand. I remembered the song *Jesus loves the little children, all the little children of the world.* Was I one of them? I sang it as loud as I could between hysterical yowling. Neighbors from next door and across the street began arriving. In summer all windows were open and few people had large fans or air conditioners. It was easy to hear conversations or a family fight, and this sounded like murder.

The daybed was finally moved, and I was pulled out in a state of shock. Uncle Maple was ordered to the kitchen. He looked bewildered by what had happened. A discussion ensued as I lay whimpering in Auntie Mae's lap. Should the doctor be called? No, warm Ovaltine and a nap was prescribed by all!!

I recovered, but I don't know about Uncle Maple. Ann said he never used his razor strap nor his belt on her again.

***

While in college, I would take the train to Carbondale and Uncle Maple and Uncle Mark would take me quail hunting. I would wear an old heavy plaid shirt and boots. One afternoon, we were following an old Indian trail through the brush. I was leading. There, in front of me was a magnificent red fox. Uncle Mark said, "shoot 'em, Bub," but I just stood and looked at that fox. (My mother once said that I looked like a fox.) The fox got up and moved into the trees.

A family gathering in southern Illinois with all members present except my mother. I am holding the gun (to the far right) before Uncle Maple and Uncle Mark took me quail hunting. I shot four quail.

That was my last quail hunt with Uncle Maple and Uncle Mark, but I loved them both.

I learned the *dog paddle* that summer in Herrin and I have continued to swim for eight decades. There was a magical place in Herrin called White City. It boasted of rides, a large swimming pool, even a roller coaster, but I was too young to ride it. Since I wasn't six until November, I could get into the park free.

Ann and I carried old towels. She knew an attendant and when he was on duty, we both got into the pool free. That saved five cents, which was a fortune in 1930. The little extra money went into a postal savings book that converted into a bond. The bond was cashed-in for college ten years later.

Knowing my weak kidneys, Ann was told to be sure I didn't pee in the pool. I didn't. However, on the way home, we had to walk seven blocks and that was too far for me. I became desperate and decided to wee-wee behind some bushes in front of this grand home that was even larger than the grandparents' house in Watseka. Surely, a house that large would have an indoor toilet and I wanted to see one of them again.

I marched up to the front door, twisted the ringer and explained to the mayor's wife exactly what my problem was, including the history of bed-wetting. Ann was mortified, the mayor's wife was amused, and I was escorted to this wonderful bathroom. It had soft tissue, not an old Sears catalog that scratched the bottom.

Auntie Mae went to the mayor's residence to apologize for her niece, explaining why I was in Herrin, which seemed, to me, to have nothing to do with my kidney problem. I had to return to Mrs. Mayor's house and apologize too. Ann took me. She didn't want to go, but we did. I wasn't afraid and I was really sorry if I offended the lady, but as I explained again to the mayor's wife that I had asked politely (out of necessity), and my table manners were very good. I had been to tea many times with grownups and I had ridden the Illinois Central train all by myself. I think she was impressed. Ann just wanted to get out of there. I was hoping for an invitation to tea, but it was not to be.

The only other exciting occurrence that summer was in the middle of the night. The "honey wagon" dumped its collection from all the outdoor privies in the middle of Herrin's main street. For some reason, the horse bolted and the driver was thrown under the stinky pile of human feces. He never recovered. The town council decided on sewers. For months, maybe years, the smell remained, especially after a rain. Of course the kids, always fascinated with what the body produces, stood on the sidewalk watching the cleanup and making appropriate remarks.

For me, it was a "larky" summer.

But the time had come for me to go to school and my mother was well enough to retrieve me. When she arrived with several friends, I decided to assert myself. I hid in a closet. When they found me there, I tried howling again. They had to carry me kicking and wiggling out to the car.

Auntie Mae and Ann cried. I didn't want to leave. Even Uncle Maple looked sad. "Will you miss me, Auntie Mae?" I asked. As the car pulled slowly away, Auntie Mae summed up my stay:

"We are going to miss you, Bub, but it will be a good miss." My southern Illinois relatives and Mr. Zimmer were the only ones to call me Bub.

I liked to think it was a term of endearment.

Lovinia's Child: A Depression Tale

Chapter V

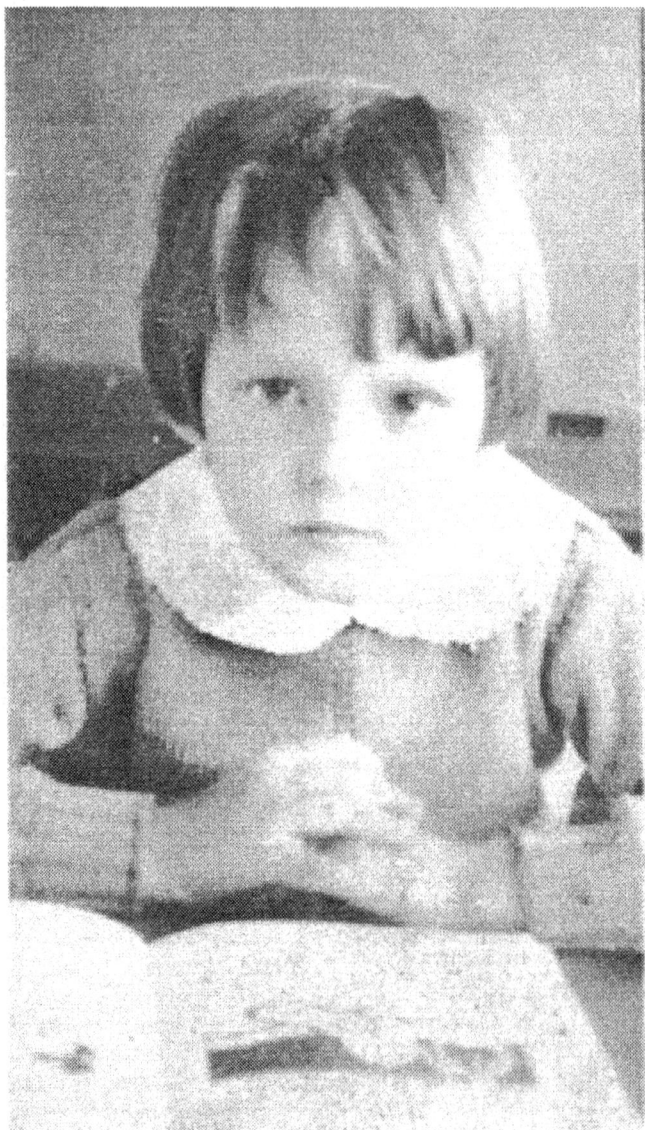

The young scholar.

There was a great difference between living in a suburb of Chicago and a small central or southern Illinois town in the 1920s. In Watseka and Herrin, everyone knew your business, your family and your secrets. The only paved street was the main street which ran past "the filling station," the garage, the appliance store, "the movie house," dress shop, the small department store and the bank. On Saturday night, people didn't buy much, but they walked up one side of the street and down the other side, stopping to visit and to share news. Watseka was a farming community. Herrin was a mining town. But they both shared Saturday nights on Main Street.

Not so in Calumet City. Saturday nights belonged to "the strip" along State Street and to the mob. You sometimes knew your neighbor if there were children on the block. Otherwise, your door was always locked and your neighbor was probably mob-related.

Thank goodness for Arnold Zimmer, my cousin Ann, and her friends, or it would have been lonely without those older playmates and the sense of belonging they temporarily gave me.

My mother and I returned to the attic apartment at the Zimmers' house in Calumet City. Arnold seemed glad to see me and Mrs. Zimmer hugged me. My mother had not been too pleased with "my deportment" as she called it, but she did not use the ivory-handled hairbrush on my backside. That came later, after she had remarried and my "doportment" had become "deplorable."

I was enrolled in Kindergarten. I loved the thought of school and of other children. Unfortunately for me and for the new teacher, I could read, probably better than she did. All we did in class was draw pictures. I cannot draw. My pictures were terrible so I scribbled words, some bad, all over my ugly drawings.

How to escape? That's when I became a runaway.

To accomplish my first escape, I took the big wooden beads that we were forced to string into big ugly necklaces, and threw them out the window. The teacher was upset. She ordered me outside to retrieve them. The rules were very strict about five-year old children wandering the halls. We were not allowed to leave the building without a parent. My mother worried that my grandparents might kidnap me. Of course, she need not have feared that. I knew in my heart that no one wanted me.

My trip to retrieve the beads entailed leaving the heavy front door, going around the two story stone structure, and crossing the playground. Escape! I had the swings to myself. I forgot the beads. Leaving the playground, I explored the fields behind the school. They were filled with early autumn flowers, daisies, Indian Paint Brush, and snot flowers of blue. All the way to Torrence Avenue I roamed. I neglected to return to school.

Just before dark, I arrived at the Zimmers' house. The police were waiting; Mrs. Zimmer was crying; Arnold looked scared. My mother had the ivory handled hairbrush in hand.

That summer I was closely monitored. I bided my time.

There has always been exhilaration about travel and never knowing where the road would lead. And the world was out there waiting for me.

My mother decided there was something wrong with me, but what? Her solution was an IQ Test. She encouraged me by saying, "Do the best you can."

She had forgotten I could read. The test was no

problem. When it was suggested I skip a grade or two, she would reply, "Barbara overcompensates." I looked that up in the dictionary that I often carried with me. I didn't understand how it applied to me.

My mother was given a job teaching the fifth grade at Lincoln School, so that's why I entered kindergarten there and quickly moved into first grade after my first escape. Obviously, my deportment was a problem, but I embarrassed her in other ways.

The state mandated smallpox vaccinations in the 20s. I was scratched with the virus and promptly passed out cold on the kindergarten floor. When the doctor arrived, I vomited all over him. I was carried back to the attic at Zimmers where I was examined by a doctor sent by Cook County. Since no one I knew could afford a doctor, the county paid interns to help the indigent. There was also a free clinic in Calumet City, but I was too sick to be taken there.

I never understood how poor we were. When everyone you know is poor, it doesn't seem to matter. Poverty is a great leveler.

Dr. Novak checked me out. What were all those spots? The first diagnosis was German Measles. But more rashes appeared and that was the dreaded Scarlet Fever. When I began to itch, the Chicken Pox had arrived. I had all three childhood diseases at one time. It was a miracle that I didn't die.

For the Zimmers, it meant a red quarantine sign on the front door. Mr. Zimmer had carried me up the stairs, so he was quarantined for several weeks to see if he got sick. That meant no work and no money. Arnold wasn't quarantined. He had a separate downstairs bedroom and was permitted to go to school. He couldn't give me books nor go up the stairs to the attic. All my dishes were washed in scalding water. All the blinds were pulled down to darken the room and save my eyes. My mother lived downstairs; she was working, and on $60 a month, discounted 15 per cent at Goldblatts, she bought food for the family.

I don't remember the first three weeks. I heard Dr. Novak tell Mrs. Zimmer,

"If she lives for the next two weeks, she may make it, but don't tell her mother."

Dr. Novak came every day. Mrs. Zimmer put cold packs on my head when my temperature soared, bathed me and sang me to sleep with German lullabies when I was restless. When I itched, Mrs. Zimmer sewed white cotton mittens that tied at the wrists so I couldn't scratch. She seemed undaunted by all of my childhood diseases. No one caught anything from me.

At some point, I first became aware of the passing of time. It was autumn and the leaves were turning when my eyes were covered. Winter came and I could hear the wind pushing the attic windows. Dr. Novak let me see, briefly, the first snow covering the branches of a big tree at the side of the house. Would I live to see the spring flowers? Later, I could hear the rains of March beating on the attic roof.

Arnold walked the eight blocks to the forest preserve and brought back roots of sassafras for tea. Nothing tasted good except the warm sassafras tea. I was really a skinny child, but I became skeletal.

Finally, the eye patches were removed. Green appeared along the tree branches and a robin sat on the windowsill.

I had not been able to read for almost eight months. Children from the first grade sent me pictures of red hearts they cut and pasted and colored, but no books.

Dr. Novak was steadfast. He checked me every week, every month, then every year until I went to college.

I spent the summer recovering. I don't remember my sixth birthday, but I was alive and that was a sufficient gift. As I became stronger, Arnold and I would walk to the grocery store on Wentworth. He would take my hand and help me across the busy street. Then, one day I could jump down the curb and run across the street.

On a pleasant morning in August, Arnold and I decided to supplement our food supply. Dressed in knickers and old shirts, dragging burlap bags behind us, we walked out of Calumet City and into the countryside near Lansing where we knew there were truck farms. By the time we got to the first truck farm, we were tired but we marched up to the front door. We asked the farmer's wife if we could dig in her field for some potatoes or onions and did she have an old chicken?

She thought about that for a while, then disappeared around the corner of the house. We sat on the steps and rested. When she came back, she had a chicken by the neck.

"Here we are," she said, as she twisted the chicken's neck, right there in front of us. Arnold stuffed it into his burlap, took me by the hand and pushed me out the front gate so I could get sick on the road. We made it home, but I couldn't eat supper that night. I had visions of dead chicken. They feasted on that old chicken for a week, and then the bones became chicken soup. I ate dill pickles.

***

The second grade was more interesting than kindergarten. There was a piano in the room, which Miss Helen beat upon with great fervor. We sang most of the time. Everything written by Stephen Foster, new ballads that are today's classics, ragtime, early Irving Berlin, and operettas (these were the best). In and out of tune, we sang joyfully. No one learned anything, but there were no discipline problems either.

After my mother had been at Lincoln School for eighteen months, we took another train trip to southern Illinois for food. Carrying burlap bags to Uncle John's farm, she again made a deal with the conductors to share what we gathered for a ticket back to Chicago. Uncle John and his wife, Maybelle, helped us stash corn, potatoes and green beans in four burlap bags, two of which went to the conductors on the home trip.

Back at Zimmers, we ate well for a long time.

My mother became something of a hero that year because it took courage to do what she did. She was a better teacher than a mother. She had done that bit with her sisters and brother. At Lincoln School she was faced with dirty, undernourished, hungry fifth graders whose parents did not understand the concept of a good breakfast in order for children to do well in school. This was 1931 and milk was a luxury.

At the same time, farming prices in Cook County were at an all-time low. So low that the cooperatives were dumping milk. Those farmers who didn't comply were stopped at the county line. Either the milk was dumped or the cans were shot up and the milk poured about on the road. When she saw this, my mother decided this waste was not to be tolerated when there were hungry children.

On Saturday morning, just after sunrise, she took me by the hand and we walked to the roadblock, near the county line, where she begged for the milk for students.

It was the only time I ever heard her beg. She didn't even beg the judge for my custody, the grandparents did that.

"Bring it to Lincoln School, pour it into hungry children, not adults, but children beginning with kindergarten, then the ascending grades one to eight." She was threatened, but no one shoved her, and all five feet-one inch of her held her ground. She actually ordered the men to be in front of Lincoln Elementary School at 8 a.m., Monday morning. Then we turned around and marched back to Zimmers.

She informed the principal, a bachelor, who said he used newspapers between the blankets to keep warm and sold Prestone on the side to pay the rent, to be ready for the milk trucks. A message went to all the teachers:

"Students must bring a large cup or glass for milk on

Monday."

On Monday morning my mother was there, lining up kids, glasses in hand, waiting for milk. You didn't have to like milk, but it was good for you.

Promptly at 8 a.m., three milk trucks came around the corner and parked in front of the school. They ladled milk until every kid had one or two glasses of fresh milk. Sometimes parents came with pitchers and those were filled. Every morning until the end of the school year, the trucks were there. I should have told her how proud I was of her. Now it is too late.

Chapter VI

The fifth grade class at Lincoln Elementary School in Calumet City in the mid-1930s. There were immigrants from 12 different European countries represented in this classroom. That explains the "mature" looks of some of the students as they had to master English before progressing to other grades.

I loved the summer when I was seven. Arnold loaned me his books. Somehow, we had plenty of food from the garden and a chicken once in a while. However, three shocks awaited me before the summer was over.

My mother remarried, and she didn't ask me or tell me until it was done. I had met Charles several times when he would pick her up for dinner. I didn't mind because I always got hamburgers with the Zimmers when she was gone.

She didn't say, "This is your new father."

She just said, "This is my husband."

I decided to hate him and to make his life miserable for taking my mother away just when I was beginning to like her. I succeeded. Charles was a good person. He later paid for camps and college and a set of the World Books. He loved my mother so I was included in the caring, but not the loving. Did she love Charles? I don't know. She took excellent care of him, and forced me to respect him, which eventually I did. He was a railroad engineer on the old Indiana Harbor-Belt. As a thirty-year veteran, he had the first diesel in the U.S. When he said it was OK, the railroad bought more. However, there was a terrible accident with the new diesel. When he left his cab to crawl under the engine to find the problem, it rolled over him. He almost died. My mother learned to drive so she could be at the hospital every day. He lived and I was glad. It took a long time for me to repay him for my indifference and misbehavior.

He did drive us to Southern Illinois on holidays to see my mother's sisters and her brother, John. We drove in style. Charles had purchased a Hupmobile. What a car! It was shiny black and as long as today's limos. His initials in gold were on the two front doors. It had a jump seat, but I preferred the whole back seat. At that time, it was the grandest thing on the road. As we would drive through central Illinois towns on our way south, people would come out of drugstores and garages to stare at that Hupmobile. We were familiar with garages because the car's axles would break frequently, and to replace them meant a trip to Chicago while we stayed the night in some small hotel where everyone believed we were part of the mob family.

Always we were treated royally in the one-car towns.

The summer of 1932, we were caught in a real tornado. Charles drove the car down into a deep ditch by the side of the road. We sat there looking up, while whole fences, parts of barns and houses were carried above us by the force of the wind. The Hupmobile didn't budge. It took two tractors and a tow truck to move the car because of its weight. No wonder the axles cracked. I cried when Charles traded it in on a more practical car. It was a friend.

**

"I'm going to live with my father," forgetting he didn't want me and even refused to acknowledge my legitimacy. I was written out of the Illinois Blue Book and the daughter of the dumpy beautician was written into the social register of sorts. Later, at age 11, when I needed a bicycle for school, eleven blocks away, he sent me a check for a pair of skates. His lawyer sent me a letter when I was on the threshold of college, stating I could receive $100 for tuition and books if I would never use the Gilbreath name again. Also, that ended child support, which had never been paid anyway. My mother had had him jailed once for non-payment, but that didn't work. She would tell me I looked just like him and often acted like him. Neither statement was meant to be a compliment. When people told me I was pretty, I knew it wasn't true.

***

The second shock came when we moved from Zimmers to Elizabeth Street. There I had my own room, but my mother had decorated the house in dark colors and the bed was too high. I was forbidden to sit on it anyway, so that didn't matter. I didn't wet the bed any more; instead, I became a nail biter and continued to run away.

I would walk to Wentworth Avenue, and then I would ride the bus free to the South Shore train station, telling the driver my father would pick me up at the station. I was a liar, too. Then I would slip behind a family with children and blend in with the group. Children rode free, and I was a small seven year-old. From Hammond into Chicago and to my goal which at first was the old Chicago Library. When I discovered the Field Museum, that was it. I wanted to live in the basement with the Egyptian mummies.

I knew about Egypt from Mr. Layer's library and especially about the mummies.

Since they were well preserved for their future life, maybe they would get up and walk around the museum at night. I had to know. After seeing the mummies, reading about them was not enough. One afternoon, I hid behind the door of the pharaoh's small room, maybe a Ramses. There were plenty of them. I took a nap propped up behind the door. The small cells were glass except for the wooden doors, so the guard checking on the mummies could not see a sleeping child behind the door. When I woke up, the visitors had gone and the lights were dim. That was fine with me. I owned the entire Egyptian collection! I went from room to room. I inspected every aspect of Egyptian life from the painted sarcophagi to the jewelry. Then I went to sleep again beside one of the mummies.

The police, the curator, my mother and the guards found me there at 4 a.m. waiting for the resurrection, which had not occurred. I was hungry and excited. Everyone else was furious.

I was house bound. The museum set a special watch for me. My mother used the ivory-handled hairbrush, which left black and blue marks on my behind. And the third shock of my seventh year was pronounced:

"You have been enrolled in a private school."

No need to tell me what kind of school that was. I knew I would hate it.

Mrs. Humphrey's Private School was for "difficult children." Her only requirement for acceptance was a minimum IQ of 125, which I was told all eleven of us had.

The first day she faced us, she said the magic words, Field Museum and mummies.

"Every other Saturday we will be going to Chicago to visit the Art Institute and the Oriental School. We will have tea at Marshall Fields and sail down the Chicago River. But you have to behave and mind your manners."

We learned self-discipline and academic discipline with Mrs. Humphrey. We received books on demand. My only problem with the Museum after that was avoiding recognition by the guards. I would pretend to blow my nose with a big handkerchief when they walked by our little group.

We put on plays, which we wrote, for the neighborhood. We went on exploring expeditions looking for butterflies and worms in the forest preserve.

Mrs. Humphrey opened up the world for us and I believe we did her proud.

She divided us into grade groupings. I was placed in third/fourth grade. Billy, later a prominent Chicago lawyer, and Edgar, a genius and later one of the world's richest men, were in fifth/sixth. Robert became a world class sailor. All of us went on to college and received advanced degrees. It was the best time I ever had in school, including graduate studies.

When Mrs. Humphrey's husband became sick, she closed the school and moved to Peoria. I was returned to public school. I entered Lincoln Elementary School again in the fourth grade. Once again, I was fortunate in having good teachers. Miss Strocko taught Greek History in the fourth grade and Roman History in the fifth. Adding to Egyptian History, was my knowledge of the Trojan War, Punic Wars, gods, goddesses, Herodotus, Caesar, Thucydides, the Roman Republic, the Roman Empire and books on all of these.

When I was sick, I memorized the World Book and discovered the Sumerians, Babylonians and Assyrians.

Years later, I found a book of quotations from Roman history, which I had underlined. They seem applicable today:

Caesar: When his friends advised him to have a bodyguard, he said, "It is better to die once than to live always in fear of death."

Cicero: "Any man who holds a state office must make it his first care that everyone shall have what belongs to him and that private citizens shall suffer no invasion of their rights by act of the state."

Livy on the Roman Republic: "Romans were one people in the world who would fight for others' liberties at their own cost. However, misunderstandings between the liberators and the liberated, in time, convinced most Greeks that the Romans were still semi-barbarians."

Livy again: He described the dark dawning of one modern day when "we can no longer endorse our vices nor face the remedies needed to cure them."

In geography class, I loved maps and could find any country in the world. I knew I had to see them, never knowing I would visit most of them one day. The greatest English teacher, Miss Cronin, trained a generation of Chicago editors. At one time, fourteen of them were working for various newspapers in and around Chicago.

It was in her fifth grade English class that I fell madly in love. When Tommy Schaffer walked through the door, the angels sang and the world stood still. Honest. Ironically, he looked like Uncle Maple with his jet-black hair, his shark grin, and his mischievous eyes. I even got a friend to make fudge for me to give to him. He went to her house after that to get fudge directly. Connie's mother liked him too, and since he lived on our street, she picked him up on the way to school. I walked. I hoped he would join the ballroom dancing class and walk me to Hohman Avenue to the studio, but his father decided that it was not a manly pursuit.

Instead, Edgar's mother told my mother that he would

walk me. I know, I know, I was told often enough that Edgar would be a success in the world, etc., etc. Of course he was. Rich and famous in the OSS during WWII, even MI-6, owning castles in Ireland, even beloved of the English aristocracy. But he danced like an elephant at thirteen and he was in love with the tiny redheaded dance teacher. She was about 4' 11" and he was 6' 3" and overweight.

I was stuck on Tommy from the fourth grade to the eighth grade, through high school and college. He married someone else. I even went to the fiftieth high school reunion just to see him again. So did six other women. He never showed up.

Several of the girls in the seventh grade who lived on Elizabeth Street went to the Presbyterian church across the state line in Hammond, since there was no Protestant church in Calumet City. The church had once belonged to the Baptists who dunked you and held you under until you saw Jesus. This was my understanding. I knew how big the dunking pool was because Charles played golf with the red faced Baptist minister until he had a stroke on the golf course after breaking several clubs over the head of his caddy.

The Presbyterians weren't much better. The minister talked on and on until people fell asleep. He also browbeat his wife in front of worshipers. I tried Sunday school but was ostracized by a prissy lady and the other girls in the class because I lived in Calumet City. I decided early on that Christianity was not for me, especially as practiced by Baptists and Presbyterians.

***

Lincoln School was not considered an outstanding school, but compared to Thornton Fractional Township High School of Calumet City, Illinois, it was absolutely great. There had been a sense of community at Lincoln. In seventh and eighth grade, you were responsible for students in the lower grades. Boys wore white belts and became patrol officers. Girls were hall monitors and in charge of grades 4, 5, and 6. It was a special goal to take our place among those in charge, or to maintain the playground I had once traversed as a runaway.

When it came time to go to high school, any student whose parents could afford it, even those who could not, went anywhere but Thornton Fractional Township High School. Even Thornton Township did not want Calumet City in its district. Besides, it was in Cook County, home of the mob. Since my mother was now teaching across the state line in Hammond, Indiana, she pleaded with me to go there.

I refused to be associated with those snobs who went to the Presbyterian Church, and who my mother considered to be "nice girls."

Did I learn anything in four years at Thornton Fractional?

At thirteen, I taught ninth grade English for Miss Jaacks who was more comfortable teaching biology and basketball.

In a high school not noted for its academic achievements, sports dominated. To be involved socially or culturally, you had to swim, play basketball or volleyball, and letter in your junior year. Heaven help the weak, disabled, or overweight.

I avoided confrontation with Mrs. Canoga, the eighty-year-old history teacher when she obviously was wrong about history. I even paid her a courtesy call because her home was filled with fabulous antiques, which I wanted to see. She was without a sense of humor when, as seniors, we presented her with a bottle of Carter's Little Liver Pills to improve her disposition. That's what the manufacturers stated it would do. She was furious and threatened to blackball us from National Honor Society. Cooler heads prevailed and we apologized.

In 1940, as the war was looming, my mother, Charles, and I moved to Lansing, Illinois, a truck farming community known for onions. Some of us earned money for the University by picking onions for twenty-five cents an hour and all of the onions we could eat in the field. We lived on the wrong side of Torrence Avenue, so I had to go, still, to Thornton Fractional Township High School of Calumet City, Illinois, not to Thornton Township.

The bus picked students up at 7 a.m. and dropped us off near the band room where we waited until classes began at 9 a.m. It was hoped by school administrators that we would use this time for studying, however, this did not happen. Without supervision, the sleepy students, now awake, threw their lunches at each other, yelled curses, and behaved in a general disorderly fashion.

What followed this behavior were two policemen and a "juke box" in the band room, which required twenty-five cents to play. That was a good thing. From another bus came Gordon with fifty cents. After six decades, I can hear Glenn *Miller's Sunrise Serenade* and remember twirling across the band room floor with Gordon at 7:30 in the morning.

I had to ride the last bus home every night so I could run track and swim after basketball practice, and win a letter in my junior year.

I liked my time alone running and swimming. At the

University, I would run early in the morning at the Armory across from the sorority house. There, I met the co-captains of the track team, Gonzales and Young. Buddy Young encouraged me in the high jump, but I was a better swimmer. I worked out with Tor Melan from Norway, the swim coach, aiming for the 1944 Olympics. Unfortunately, especially for the Finnish people, the Russians bombed Helsinki that year and the Olympics were not held. In 1948, I was pregnant with my first child and too old for competition. But Buddy Young took home lots of gold, and I could tell everyone that we ran together when I was a sophomore at the University.

***

We had a mediocre football team at Thornton Fractional Township High School. No one thought cheerleading was a worthy endeavor. And how do you make something lyrical out of a song about Thornton Fractional Township High School? So our solution and our unofficial fight song became the *Beer Barrel Polka*. It was played at all school functions, including Friday night socials held in the gym.

It was played at graduation.

At the university, it became embarrassing when, as a sorority pledge, I was called upon to sing the school song. Everyone knew I came from Calumet City. Edgar, the genius at Mrs. Humphrey's school would tell his Harvard classmates that he went to the Thornton Academy in Chicago. There is no Thornton Academy in Chicago.

The summer of 1938 was a peaceful, routine time. Although the "silver shirts" (American Nazis) marched down Michigan Boulevard in Chicago and stories of prison camps for dissidents in Germany filtered down to the reading public, there was really no concern except for a few Jewish families worried about relatives. My best friend, Florence, and I talked about boys, the new high school in the fall, clothes, etc. Her parents owned a small department store and worried about swastikas painted on the sidewalk in front of the store.

Mrs. Lynn asked me to join the family when they went to a cottage in the Dunes Park, near Gary, Indiana. I ate kosher for the first time since I left Grandmother's house in Watseka. We had lox and bagels and all kinds of good things. We wore bathing suits all day, swam in Lake Michigan, and went to sandy beds at night. It was a happy time. For years, I never realized the problems confronted by Florence and her family. My grandmother had protected her children from discrimination and my mother protected me. To be Jewish and Native American in or near Chicago in 1938 was difficult, and that is an understatement.

***

On December 7, 1941, the whole world changed overnight. Pearl Harbor was a defining event in my world. The following week, most of the boys in the senior class had enlisted in the army or the navy. The next week, the junior class was smaller. Then the men teachers and the bus drivers left. We hitched rides to school, standing at the bus stops in the morning and hiking home at night, but always in twos or threes.

Rationing was required for meat, butter, and shoes. My mother gave me her stamps for my first pair of black high-heeled shoes. I didn't have a pair of hose until I was nineteen. We chewed lots of bubble gum to line the inside of tires, because there was no rubber. The Japanese controlled the rubber when they took over the French possessions in Vietnam.

Once again, only the mob had access to sugar and gas. State Street was alive with the military. The men celebrated before going to Europe and really celebrated their return home. The wounded would get free booze on "the strip." The mob was patriotic. But those who "skimmed," died. The favorite method of punishment in the 40s was the garrote, as the father of one of my friends discovered. His body turned up in a sewer near the state line. It was said that he "skimmed" sugar. However, later on Christmas Eve when we brought small gifts for the family, there was a knock on the front door. No one moved for thirty seconds. When Mrs. V. opened the front door, there piled in the snow, were boxes filling the front porch: albums of opera, toys for the baby, perfume and scarfs for the girls, sports equipment for Angie's brother. No gift cards were attached, but we knew who had brought them. This was "*la familia.*"

The time had come for everyone to be involved in the war effort. Selling stamps and helping entertain troops at the service centers didn't seem sufficient. I had heard about women pilots volunteering to ferry planes. Their headquarters was near Amarillo. It was time to run away again, this time to Texas.

Just before my sixteenth birthday, I went to the small Lansing Airport where I had been taking flying lessons. With a small bag containing my new high-heeled, black shoes and lots of lipstick, I believed I looked nineteen, at least.

I really got to Texas. The lady pilots took one look at me, when I said I could fly, and asked one question,

"How old are you?"

I lied.

When I was sent back to Lansing, several days later, I

was grounded until graduation.

But at the University, my past helped me find a way to fly and help the war effort. I became an "airplane spotter." Chanute Field was near Urbana and so were all those pilots eager to advance my education. The first university airport was constructed almost in my backyard. When the runways were poured, an aeronautical engineering course was offered for teachers of aeronautics. And part of the program included flying time at our new airport where Chanute pilots could practice landings and take-offs.

As a member of the *Daily Illini*, I could offer pictures and publicity, and that's how I joined this special class. I passed all the tests, including aircraft maintenance and navigation to everyone's amazement. My secret: On Saturday morning in a pair of short shorts and a red, red sleeveless top, I would hike to the airport and wait until pilots would land in their AT-6s. I was always invited to fly. I was teachable. I even flew a P-38.

On the day the University of Illinois Airport officially opened, I covered the big story. Later, when the crowds dispersed, Captain Gentile, a WWII ace, took me up in his plane. We flew over the V-12 dormitories pretending to dive-bomb the buildings. The local FAA received calls demanding to know if the war had ended or if the university was being attacked. Captain Gentile crashed some years later. Time has not dimmed the memory of that fall afternoon when he took me for the ride of my life.

***

Back home, although grounded, I was permitted to join a small high school sorority. For our initiation, the sorority decided to do something about civic virtue. Blindfolded, armed with toothbrushes and a pail of soapy water, we were taken to State Street and "the strip."

There, we were ordered to "clean it up." Scrub down the entrance to each tavern and strip joint with our toothbrushes.

The police were not amused, nor were the tavern owners, our parents, and the school. Underage girls NOT drinking or performing, would NOT be tolerated. Our parents were called. Everyone appeared to be mortified. Tavern owners especially, because their tax money paid for Thornton Fractional Township High School and for our books.

We were a close-knit group in the sorority, especially after we had "cleaned up State Street." Many of us worked because that was a necessity if we wanted to go to college. At fifteen, a social security card was available. That enabled a young person to make twenty-five cents an hour minimum wage. Of course, some businesses cheated and only paid seventeen or eighteen cents an hour if you were fifteen or sixteen.

I was lucky in clerking first at Goldblatts Department Store where we received a 10% discount on most things they carried, excluding food. At age six, I could remember going with my mother to cash her teacher's check there. Goldblatts was the only store in town to pay 60% of the check. No one believed the state of Illinois could make good on $80 during the Depression. Check cashing was done in the basement of the store. With me tagging along, we would walk down a long hallway with policemen against the wall on one side. On the other side were food tables with fresh bread, meats, and desserts. At the end of the hall was the cashier's cage. After trying to ignore the smell of baking bread and hot coffee when you were hungry, and there were times we were hungry, I believed Goldblatts owed me a job.

The county seemed to be coming out of the Depression when World War II began. Who knows if it was a result of New Deal programs or European Allies buying war materials from the United States. At seventeen there was planning for college, the university and clothes for "rush week." That summer I had a wonderful job at Fox and Sons. I never met the senior Fox, but his sons had a men's store in

Hammond, Indiana where state legislators, winning football coaches and prominent citizens went to be suited. And I selected their ties.

This was a classy operation and I learned about style from the brothers Fox. I received a 20% discount on the small, select collection for women and was able to buy a three-quarters Lynx coat from one of the Fox daughters. I wore that coat four seasons of the year. No one had a coat like it. And I wondered why my sorority sisters thought my family had money, although I worked three jobs and sometimes went to class. But before I could enroll at the university, I needed permission from Judge Pozanski because I was still a ward of the court.

The courthouse on the corner of Wentworth looked the same. I had managed to avoid it after the custody fight thirteen years before. It had been in all the newspapers in Hammond and Chicago, but my mother had burned them all.

In the judge's office, I tried to look sure of myself and very grown up. I wore my black high heels with ankle straps and gold trim. The judge must have thought so, too. He didn't ask me how old I was. He looked old and his eyes were tired.

"This calls for a celebration. I heard you did well in

high school." (I had done very well).

He opened his desk drawer, took out two shot glasses and a bottle of whiskey. I prayed that it wasn't something that Mr. Zimmer and I had concocted.

"Drink up, kid," and he tossed off his whiskey.

He poured a second shot as I sat there debating what to do with the first. I imitated him. I thought my throat would disintegrate.

While he poured himself a third shot, I excused myself and ran to the restroom. After being sick, I took the elevator to the main floor. I never looked back. I never saw Judge Pozanski again. Maybe I am still a ward of the court in Cook County, Illinois. I hope not.

I did return to Calumet City and to Thornton Fractional with Florence for the fiftieth reunion of our graduation class, many of whom were dead or in prison. Had anything changed? After fifty years, the combination on my locker was the same. The swimming pool where I had first learned my winning backstroke was filled-in. The interior of the building was painted a sickly puce color. There were now several outbuildings and a cinder parking lot with some old cars that probably belonged to the teachers.

We did not tour "the strip" on State Street.

Most people who might remember me are gone, so I

can tell you what it was like without recrimination nor guilt which, most of us carry for one reason or another.

I had survived my childhood, the Depression, and Calumet City. I understand it has become a rather respectable place, but not as lively as it was, once upon a tale.

Signed,

Lovinia's Child

Texas, 2005

Words

"Most people quit too early."
John Melankamp in a television interview.

"Ever insurgent let me be.
Make me more daring than devout.
From sleek contentment keep me free,
And fill me with a buoyant doubt.
From compromise and things half done,
Keep me, dear Lord, with stern and stubborn pride.
And when at last the fight is won,
God, keep me still unsatisfied." *Anonymous*

"I'll lay me down and rest a while.
And then I'll rise and fight again."
Matthew Arnold

"Pain that cannot forget, draws drop by drop upon the heart, until in our despair, there comes wisdom through the awesome Grace of God."
Aeschylus